ON
BOARD

On Board

13-Digit ISBN: 978-1-64643-171-7
10-Digit ISBN: 1-64643-171-5

This book may be ordered by mail from the publisher. Please include $5.99 for postage and handling. Please support your local bookseller first!

Books published by Cider Mill Press Book Publishers are available at special discounts for bulk purchases in the United States by corporations, institutions, and other organizations. For more information, please contact the publisher.

Cider Mill Press Book Publishers
"Where good books are ready for press"
PO Box 454
12 Spring Street
Kennebunkport, Maine 04046

Visit us online!
cidermillpress.com

Typography: Operetta B, Filson Pro, IvyPresto Text
Image Credits: All photos courtesy of Derek Bissonnette

Printed in China
1 2 3 4 5 6 7 8 9 0
First Edition

ON BOARD

INSPIRATION,
IDEAS & RECIPES
FOR EXCEPTIONAL
ENTERTAINING

DEREK BISSONNETTE
GABRIELLE COTE

CIDER MILL
PRESS

BOOK
PUBLISHERS
KENNEBUNKPORT, MAINE

Contents

Introduction

It's great to have options—until you have so many that making a definitive decision becomes an insurmountable challenge.

The serving board is one of those spots where the choices available are so plentiful that they quickly become overwhelming. When one starts to think about all of the delicious cheeses, charcuterie, fruits, spreads, dips, nuts, and comforting nibbles that can fill up an empty board, the mind starts to reel. With so many possibilities, it becomes difficult to simply settle for a series of delicious bites that will make people happy. Instead, we tend to try and use this plenty to compose something perfect, something that will leave others in awe. Inevitably, as we become inclined toward faultlessness, we falter.

This book intends to provide you with a reliable set of approaches to return to whenever you're struggling to navigate the innumerable options available. This set of composed serving boards will teach you how to capture the magic available in each season, how to successfully execute a theme, how to outfit your boards so that their appearance is as pleasant as the taste of the items on them, and, most importantly, how to prepare simple but inventive offerings that will transform every occasion where you entertain into a memorable, and manageable, one. To do this, we break down each item on a board so that you can learn what flavors go best together. We continually emphasize the importance of selecting the very best ingredients, and also show you how to dress up those items that are already familiar to people and would otherwise fail to elicit much enthusiasm.

Once you have this foundation, you'll feel more confident about tailoring boards to your own preferences, and those of your guests. You'll start to focus on the freshest ingredients available at the market, and let them do most of the heavy lifting, following their lead when deciding how to fill up the rest of the space on a board. If need be, you can always return to the safety of these boards. But the hope is that you only come back for inspiration.

Spring

The return of warmth and vibrant life to the world should be celebrated as often as possible. These boards help you do just that, pushing fresh, bold flavors at every opportunity, and keeping it simple so that you can soak up every ounce of loveliness available.

Lemon & Thyme Board

The two flavors lending their names to this board form the perfect bridge from the austere winter to the hopeful brightness of spring.

A ## THYME & ASIAGO CRACKERS

The light, citrusy flavor of thyme forms the bridge between its strong earthiness and the Asiago in these crackers.

B ## LEMON RICOTTA

Simply put, one of the most delightful combinations known to man. You'll be looking to find a spot for this on many of your boards.

C ## DRY ITALIAN SALAMI

A serving board staple with good reason.

D ## HONEYCOMB

This is becoming easier and easier to find, a testament to its universal appeal.

Lemon Ricotta

YIELD: 2 Cups
ACTIVE TIME: 10 Minutes
TOTAL TIME: 3 Hours

INGREDIENTS

4 cups whole milk

Juice of 2 lemons

1 tablespoon kosher salt

DIRECTIONS

1. Place the milk in a saucepan and warm it over medium heat until it is just about to come to a boil (about 190°F). Remove the pan from heat, add the lemon juice, and stir for 1 minute. Cover the pan and let the mixture stand for 15 minutes. This will allow the curds to separate.

2. Ladle the curds into cheesecloth, tie it with kitchen twine, and let it drain at room temperature until almost all of the liquid has drained, about 2½ hours. Stir the salt into the ricotta and serve.

Thyme & Asiago Crackers

YIELD: 15 Crackers
ACTIVE TIME: 10 Minutes
TOTAL TIME: 1 Hour

INGREDIENTS

4 oz. unsalted butter

1 cup freshly grated Asiago cheese

Zest of 1 lemon

2 tablespoons chopped fresh thyme

1¼ cups all-purpose flour, plus more as needed

½ teaspoon kosher salt

¼ teaspoon black pepper

DIRECTIONS

1. Place all of the ingredients in a food processor and pulse until the mixture comes together as a dough.

2. Place the dough on a flour-dusted work surface and roll it into a 2-inch log. Cover tightly with plastic wrap and chill in the refrigerator for 30 minutes.

3. Preheat the oven to 350°F and line two baking sheets with parchment paper. Remove the dough from the refrigerator, cut it into ½ inch thick slices, and place them on the baking sheet.

4. Place in the oven and bake until the crackers are golden brown, about 12 minutes. Remove from the oven and let the crackers cool before serving.

Thyme & Asiago Crackers
see page 15

Farmers Market Board

The spring return to the local farmers market has become a new, welcome spring tradition. This board helps you make the most of that early bounty.

A CRUDITES

Any vegetable you like will work on this board. But the King of Spring, aka asparagus, should be included.

B VERMONT CREAMERY BIJOU CHEESE

A soft goat cheese that is surprisingly sharp and complex.

C SOPPRESSATA

A dry-cured salami that is leaner than you'd think, the flavor of soppressata will change according to which part of Italy a particular offering hails from.

D PEPPERED SALAMI

A mild cured meat, laced with just enough spice to make you sit up straight and take notice.

E PEA & PARMESAN DIP

As spring is the only time of year you can procure fresh, locally grown peas, it's good to have as many methods that utilize them as possible.

F PARMESAN CRISPS

A simple way to add crunch to a board, and a preparation that takes full advantage of Parmesan's one-of-a-kind flavor.

G BALSAMIC RANCH

It's a little bit more involved than you'd think from an initial glance, and far more delicious.

Pea & Parmesan Dip

YIELD: 2 Cups
ACTIVE TIME: 10 Minutes
TOTAL TIME: 20 Minutes

INGREDIENTS

Salt and pepper, to taste

3 cups peas

1 cup water

3 tablespoons pine nuts

1 cup freshly grated Parmesan cheese

1 garlic clove, minced

½ cup fresh mint, chiffonade

DIRECTIONS

1. Bring water to a boil in a large saucepan. Add salt and the peas and cook until they are bright green and warmed through, about 2 minutes.

2. Transfer half of the peas to a food processor. Add the water, pine nuts, Parmesan, and garlic and blitz until pureed.

3. Place the puree in a serving dish, add the peas and mint, and fold to incorporate. Season the dip with salt and pepper and chill in the refrigerator until ready to serve.

Parmesan Crisps

YIELD: 24 Crisps
ACTIVE TIME: 10 Minutes
TOTAL TIME: 25 Minutes

INGREDIENTS

2 cups freshly grated Parmesan cheese

2 tablespoons everything bagel seasoning

2 tablespoons all-purpose flour

DIRECTIONS

1. Preheat the oven to 350°F and line a baking sheet with a silpat mat. Place all of the ingredients in a food processor and blitz until combined.

2. Use a 2-inch ring mold to shape the mixture into rounds that are about ¼ inch thick.

3. Place in the oven and bake until brown and crispy, about 7 minutes. Remove from the oven and let cool before serving.

Balsamic Ranch

YIELD: 2 Cups
ACTIVE TIME: 5 Minutes
TOTAL TIME: 5 Minutes

INGREDIENTS

½ cup mayonnaise

½ cup sour cream

½ cup buttermilk

3 tablespoons balsamic vinegar

¼ teaspoon onion powder

½ teaspoon garlic powder

2 teaspoons chopped fresh parsley

DIRECTIONS

1. Place all of the ingredients in a mixing bowl and whisk until the mixture is thoroughly combined.

2. Taste, adjust the seasoning as needed, and refrigerate until ready to serve.

Strawberry Rhubarb Board

Strawberry and rhubarb makes most people think of summer, but both actually peak in the late spring. On a warm evening in early June, this board will permanently brand that fact on your brain.

A FOIE GRAS TORCHON

There's been much fuss about whether foie gras can be produced humanely. As with everything, it's dependent upon the producer. But rest assured, you can acquire it from a farm that treats its animals well.

B STRAWBERRY CHIPS

It can be tough to get the oven to a low-enough temperature to pull off dehydrating these chips properly, but they're worth experimenting with if you don't have a dehydrator.

C BELLAVITANO BALSAMIC CHEESE

A hard cows' milk cheese that is a unique hybrid of Parmesan and cheddar.

D PICKLED RHUBARB

As we all know, rhubarb is legally required to be present when strawberries show up. Pickling it puts a novel spin on the classic combo.

E PUMPERNICKEL TOAST POINTS

Any bread or cracker will do here, but the earthy, slightly sweet flavor of pumpernickel is best.

Pickled Rhubarb

YIELD: 4 Servings
ACTIVE TIME: 10 Minutes
TOTAL TIME: 2 Hours

INGREDIENTS

½ cup red wine

½ cup red wine vinegar

½ cup sugar

2 sprigs of fresh mint

Zest and juice of 1 orange

1 cup finely diced rhubarb

DIRECTIONS

1. Place the red wine, red wine vinegar, and sugar in a medium saucepan and bring it to a boil.

2. Stir in the remaining ingredients and remove the pan from heat. Pour the mixture into a sterilized mason jar and let it cool to room temperature.

3. Chill the pickles in the refrigerator for 1 hour before serving.

Strawberry Chips

YIELD: 4 Servings
ACTIVE TIME: 15 Minutes
TOTAL TIME: 3 Hours

INGREDIENTS

½ cup water

½ cup sugar

1 teaspoon pure vanilla extract

1 cup hulled and thinly sliced strawberries

DIRECTIONS

1. Place the water and sugar in a small saucepan and bring to a boil, stirring to dissolve the sugar. Stir in the vanilla, remove the pan from heat, and let the syrup cool.

2. Dip the strawberries in the syrup and place them on a parchment-lined baking sheet. Place in a food dehydrator set at 140°F and dehydrate for 1 hour.

3. Turn the strawberries over and dehydrate for another 1½ hours. Serve immediately or store in an airtight container.

Pumpernickel Toast Points

YIELD: 4 Servings
ACTIVE TIME: 5 Minutes
TOTAL TIME: 25 Minutes

INGREDIENTS

6 slices of pumpernickel bread

Extra-virgin olive oil, to taste

Salt and pepper, to taste

DIRECTIONS

1. Preheat the oven to 350°F. Remove the crusts from the slices of bread and use a rolling pin to roll them flat.

2. Cut each slice into triangles, drizzle olive oil over them, and season with salt and pepper. Place them on a baking sheet, place it in the oven, and toast until they are crispy, about 6 minutes. Remove and let cool slightly before serving.

Foie Gras Torchon

YIELD: 4 Servings
ACTIVE TIME: 15 Minutes
TOTAL TIME: 16 Hours and 15 Minutes

INGREDIENTS

1 lb. foie gras

2 cups whole milk

2 teaspoons kosher salt

2 teaspoons sugar

⅛ teaspoon pink curing salt

1 tablespoon bourbon

DIRECTIONS

1. Place the foie gras in a baking pan, cover it with the milk, and let it soak in the refrigerator for at least 8 hours and up to 24.

2. Strain and pass the foie gras through a fine-mesh sieve into a mixing bowl. Stir in the kosher salt, sugar, and curing salt and then roll the mixture into a log. Wrap the log in cheesecloth and chill in the refrigerator for 8 hours.

3. Unwrap the torchon, slice it, and let the torchon come to room temperature before serving.

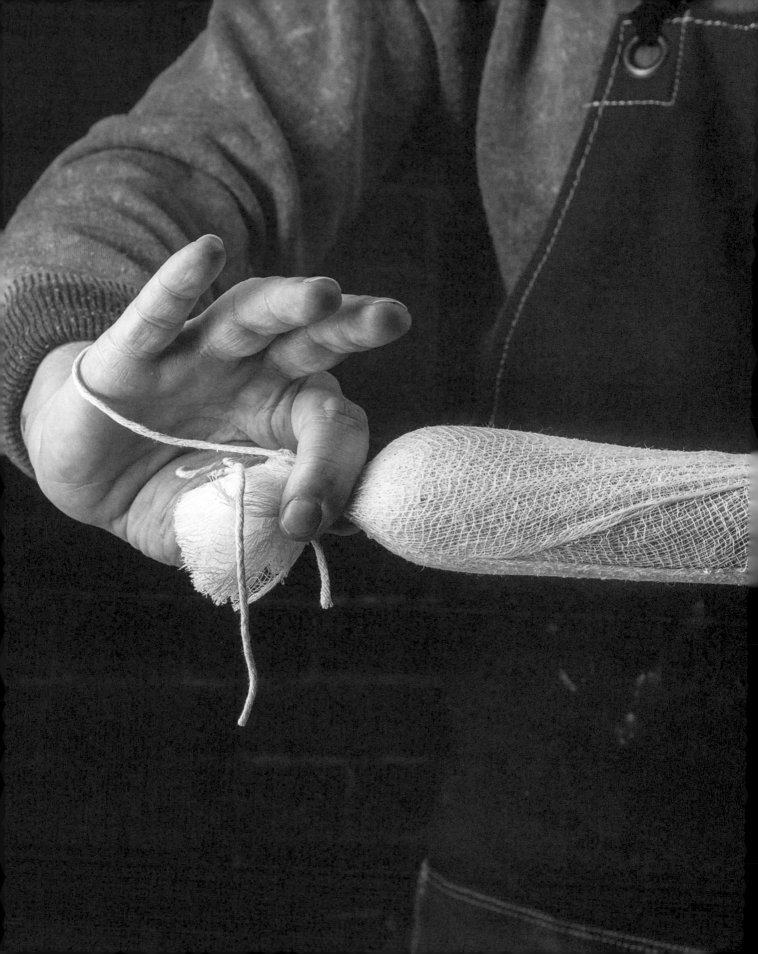

Beef Carpaccio Board

Spring is a time to savor the simple things, such as the miraculous, unbidden return of life to a world dormant for months. A board composed of thinly sliced and gently seasoned beef, the perfect flavor of Parmesan, and a garlic-enriched aioli should do much to encourage this perspective.

Ⓐ BEEF CARPACCIO

Traditionally, the beef in carpaccio is raw, but we've found that lightly searing it is an improvement.

Ⓑ PARMESAN SPHERES

A bit of focus will be necessary, but the cloud-like capsules of Parmesan that result are worth the effort.

Ⓒ ROASTED GARLIC AIOLI

You'd be wise to make extra, as you'll soon be spreading this on everything.

Ⓓ CRACKERS

Any cracker will do here, but one with an olive oil base will work best on this board.

Beef Carpaccio

YIELD: 2 Servings
ACTIVE TIME: 20 Minutes
TOTAL TIME: 1 Hour and 20 Minutes

INGREDIENTS

4 oz. beef tenderloin

Salt and pepper, to taste

1 tablespoon extra-virgin olive oil

DIRECTIONS

1. Tie the tenderloin with kitchen twine so that it will maintain its shape while it sears. Season the beef with salt and pepper.

2. Coat a skillet with the olive oil and warm it over medium-high heat. Add the tenderloin and cook, turning it as it browns, until it is seared all over. Remove the tenderloin from the pan and let it cool to room temperature.

3. Cover the tenderloin tightly with plastic wrap and freeze it for 1 hour.

4. To serve, slice the tenderloin as thin as possible.

Parmesan Spheres

YIELD: 2 Servings
ACTIVE TIME: 45 Minutes
TOTAL TIME: 1 Hour and 45 Minutes

INGREDIENTS

4 cups freshly grated Parmesan cheese

1 cup egg whites

4 cups canola oil

DIRECTIONS

1. Line a baking sheet with parchment paper. Place the cheese and egg whites in a food processor and blitz until pureed. Scoop ¼-cup portions of the puree onto the baking sheet and place it in the freezer for 45 minutes.

2. Add the canola oil to a Dutch oven and warm it to 350°F over medium heat. Working in batches, add the spheres to the oil and fry, turning occasionally, until they are golden brown, about 4 minutes. Transfer the cooked spheres to a paper towel–lined plate to drain and serve once they have all been cooked.

Roasted Garlic Aioli

YIELD: 2 Servings
ACTIVE TIME: 10 Minutes
TOTAL TIME: 40 Minutes

INGREDIENTS

1 head of garlic

½ cup extra-virgin olive oil, plus more as needed

Salt and pepper, to taste

1 egg yolk

1 teaspoon fresh lemon juice

DIRECTIONS

1. Preheat the oven to 350°F. Cut the top ½ inch of the head of garlic off. Place it in a piece of aluminum foil, drizzle olive oil over it, and season it with salt.

2. Seal the garlic in the foil, place it in the oven, and roast until the garlic cloves have softened and are caramelized, about 30 minutes. Remove from the oven, remove the cloves from the head of garlic, and place them in a mixing bowl. Mash the garlic cloves until smooth.

3. Add the egg yolk and lemon juice and whisk to combine. While whisking continually, add the olive oil in a slow steam. When all of the oil has been emulsified, season the aioli with salt and pepper and serve.

Roasted Garlic Aioli
see page 41

Mediterranean Board

Falafel is a fried dumpling full of vibrant, fresh and refreshing flavors thanks to the use of soft herbs such as parsley and cilantro, which really wake up the palette. This board is perfect for spring, with the bit of spice all you need to feel alive after hibernating all winter.

 TZATZIKI

This creamy, mint-spiked dip is a crowd-pleaser.

 FALAFEL

Dried chickpeas are the best option for these dumplings.

C LAMB MEATBALLS

The potent taste of lamb goes delightfully with a bit of the Tzatziki dabbed on top.

D GRILLED HALLOUMI

Halloumi's mild flavor and ability to withstand high temperatures makes it perfect for grilling.

 **KALAMATA OLIVES**

Never cheap out on the olives when composing a board.

F PITA BREAD

Quality pita is available at the store, but it's just as easy to make at home.

 ROASTED TOMATOES

The burst of umami provided by blistered tomatoes is the cherry atop this board.

 SPICY CHICKPEAS

These crunchy chickpeas are wonderful on a board, but they also make for a lovely, light snack.

Falafel

INGREDIENTS

1 (14 oz.) can of chickpeas, drained and rinsed

½ red onion, chopped

1 cup fresh parsley, chopped

1 cup fresh cilantro, chopped

3 bunches of scallions, trimmed and chopped

1 jalapeño pepper, stemmed, seeded, and chopped

3 garlic cloves

1 teaspoon cumin

1 teaspoon kosher salt, plus more to taste

½ teaspoon cardamom

¼ teaspoon black pepper

2 tablespoons chickpea flour

½ teaspoon baking soda

4 cups canola oil

DIRECTIONS

1. Line a baking sheet with parchment paper. Place all of the ingredients, except for the canola oil, in a food processor and blitz until pureed. Scoop ¼-cup portions of the puree onto the baking sheet and place it in the refrigerator for 1 hour.

2. Add the canola oil to a Dutch oven and warm it to 350°F over medium heat. Working in batches, add the falafel to the oil and fry, turning occasionally, until they are golden brown, about 6 minutes. Transfer the cooked falafel to a paper towel–lined plate to drain and serve once all of the falafel have been cooked.

Tzatziki

YIELD: ½ Cup
ACTIVE TIME: 10 Minutes
TOTAL TIME: 1 Hour and 10 Minutes

INGREDIENTS

1 cucumber, sliced thin

1 garlic clove, minced

1 teaspoon kosher salt

½ cup yogurt

1 tablespoon chopped fresh mint

DIRECTIONS

1. Place the cucumber, garlic, and salt in a mixing bowl and let it rest for 1 hour.

2. Strain the cucumber mixture and reserve the liquid. Place the cucumber mixture in a mixing bowl, add the yogurt and mint, and stir to combine.

3. Incorporate the reserved liquid 1 teaspoon at a time until the tzatziki has the desired texture and store in the refrigerator until ready to serve.

Falafel
see page 46

Roasted Tomatoes

YIELD: 4 Servings
ACTIVE TIME: 5 Minutes
TOTAL TIME: 30 Minutes

INGREDIENTS

12 grape tomatoes, on the vine

Olive oil, to taste

Salt and pepper, to taste

DIRECTIONS

1. Preheat the oven to 350°F. Place the tomatoes on a baking sheet, drizzle olive oil over them, and season with salt and pepper.

2. Place the tomatoes in the oven and roast until they are blistered and starting to collapse, about 10 minutes. Remove from the oven and let the tomatoes cool briefly before serving.

Lamb Meatballs

YIELD: 4 Servings
ACTIVE TIME: 20 Minutes
TOTAL TIME: 40 Minutes

INGREDIENTS

1 lb. ground lamb

1 white onion, grated

½ cup bread crumbs

1 egg

2 garlic cloves, minced

¼ cup fresh parsley, chopped

¼ cup fresh cilantro, chopped

¾ teaspoon cayenne pepper

¼ teaspoon red pepper flakes

Salt and pepper, to taste

2 tablespoons extra-virgin olive oil

DIRECTIONS

1. Place all of the ingredients, except for the olive oil, in a mixing bowl and work the mixture with your hands until combined. Form the mixture into 1-inch meatballs and chill them in the freezer for 15 minutes.

2. Place the olive oil in a large skillet and warm it over medium heat. When the oil starts to shimmer, add the meatballs to the pan and cook, turning occasionally, until they are browned all over and cooked through, about 12 minutes. Let the meatballs cool slightly before serving.

Grilled Halloumi

YIELD: 4 Servings
ACTIVE TIME: 5 Minutes
TOTAL TIME: 20 Minutes

INGREDIENTS

8 oz. halloumi cheese

Olive oil, to taste

DIRECTIONS

1. Preheat a gas or charcoal grill to 350°F. Cut the halloumi into pieces that are approximately ½ inch wide.

2. Drizzle olive oil over the cheese and place it on the grill. Grill until the cheese is warm and has grill marks on both sides, about 6 minutes. Remove from the grill and serve immediately.

Prosciutto & Melon Board

The refreshing taste of cantaloupe was made to sit beside the complex flavor of prosciutto. As this pair encourages one to kick back with a glass or two of wine—may I suggest a bottle of the always overlooked Picpoul—some pleasantly spiced nuts will help you keep your wits about you.

A MARINATED FETA

You may not be used to seeing it outside of a salad, but make a habit of tossing it on your boards.

B SICILIAN BAR NUTS

These will make for a great snack, so make a habit of whipping some up any time you're using the oven to roast or bake another preparation.

C CRISPY PANCETTA

You want to take a little bit of the chewiness out of pancetta to take full advantage of its flavor, and a brief roasting in the oven does just that.

D PROSCIUTTO & CANTALOUPE POPS

Any melon can be used, but none will be as aesthetically pleasing as cantaloupe.

Prosciutto & Cantaloupe Pops

YIELD: 4 Servings
ACTIVE TIME: 10 Minutes
TOTAL TIME: 10 Minutes

INGREDIENTS

2 cups chopped cantaloupe

4 oz. prosciutto, chopped

DIRECTIONS

1. Wrap a piece of cantaloupe in a piece of prosciutto and insert a toothpick or a wooden dowel in the bottom of the piece of cantaloupe. Repeat with the remaining cantaloupe and prosciutto.

Marinated Feta

YIELD: 4 Servings
ACTIVE TIME: 5 Minutes
TOTAL TIME: 2 Hours and 5 Minutes

INGREDIENTS

8 oz. feta cheese

1 sprig of fresh basil

¾ cup extra-virgin olive oil

½ cup white wine vinegar

2 tablespoons black pepper

1 teaspoon kosher salt

¾ teaspoon red pepper flakes

DIRECTIONS

1. Cut the feta into bite-sized chunks and place them in a mason jar.

2. Combine the remaining ingredients in a mixing bowl and then pour the marinade over the feta. Let the cheese marinate for at least 2 hours before serving.

Sicilian Bar Nuts

YIELD: 4 Servings
ACTIVE TIME: 10 Minutes
TOTAL TIME: 25 Minutes

INGREDIENTS

¾ cup walnuts

¾ cup cashews

¾ cup pecan halves

2 tablespoons unsalted butter, melted

2 tablespoons chopped fresh rosemary

1 teaspoon cayenne pepper

1 tablespoon brown sugar

1 tablespoon flaky sea salt

DIRECTIONS

1. Preheat the oven to 350°F. Place the nuts on a baking sheet, place them in the oven, and toast until fragrant, about 12 minutes. Remove from the oven and transfer the nuts to a mixing bowl.

2. Add the melted butter and toss until the nuts are evenly coated. Add the remaining ingredients, toss to coat, and serve.

Sicilian Bar Nuts
see page 63

Crispy Pancetta

YIELD: 4 Servings
ACTIVE TIME: 10 Minutes
TOTAL TIME: 40 Minutes

INGREDIENTS

3 oz. pancetta, sliced

DIRECTIONS

1. Preheat the oven to 350°F and line two baking sheets with silpat mats. Divide the pancetta between the baking sheets.

2. Place the sheets in the oven and bake the pancetta until it is browned and crispy, about 20 minutes. Remove from the oven, transfer the pancetta to a piece of parchment paper, and let cool before serving.

Summer

Summer inclines us toward joy, boisterous outings, and decadence. All that fun also has a tendency to leave us drained, and with the feeling everything is passing too quickly. Use these boards to space out the days, to slow down and spend some time appreciating the calm, quiet moments.

Peaches & Bacon Board

Blue cheese, bacon, and peaches all speak to the celebration that the summertime is. A glass of better-than-average bourbon, such as Baker's, will be the capstone.

A **BACON JAM**

Try to hold out for dry-cured bacon if you can find it, as it tends to carry a more complex flavor.

B **YOGURT & BUCKWHEAT CRACKERS**

You'd never guess by looking at its name, but buckwheat is gluten-free.

C **FIGS**

Black mission are the default variety of fig, and they'll be good here, but see if you can track down some of the less-sweet Brown Turkey figs.

D **PEACHES**

If you want to take this board up a notch, halve, pit, and char the peaches on your grill before slicing them.

E **POINT REYES BLUE CHEESE**

A rindless blue from California that rose to prominence thanks to a surprising burst of sweetness.

F **RED APPLE HICKORY SMOKED BOURBON GOUDA CHEESE**

A semi-hard cheese that features the creaminess of gouda and the smoke and sweetness of bourbon.

G **COCKTAIL ONIONS**

If bourbon's not your thing, take a cue from their inclusion to whip up a few Gibsons, that too-often-overlooked descendent of the Martini.

YIELD: ½ Cup
ACTIVE TIME: 20 Minutes
TOTAL TIME: 1 Hour

Bacon Jam

INGREDIENTS

8 oz. bacon

½ white onion, minced

1 garlic clove, minced

2 tablespoons apple cider vinegar

2 tablespoons brown sugar

1 tablespoon maple syrup

DIRECTIONS

1. Preheat the oven to 350°F. Set a wire rack in a rimmed baking sheet, place the bacon on the rack, and place the sheet in the oven. Bake the bacon until it is crispy, about 10 minutes.

2. Remove from the oven and transfer the bacon to a paper towel–lined plate to drain. Reserve the bacon fat. When the bacon is cool enough to handle, chop it into small pieces.

3. Place the reserved bacon fat in a large skillet and warm it over medium heat. Add the onion and cook, stirring frequently, until it has softened, about 5 minutes.

4. Stir in the bacon and the remaining ingredients, bring the mixture to a simmer, and cook until it has reduced slightly. Transfer the mixture to a bowl and let it chill in the refrigerator before serving.

Yogurt & Buckwheat Crackers

YIELD: 30 Crackers
ACTIVE TIME: 15 Minutes
TOTAL TIME: 1 Hour and 30 Minutes

INGREDIENTS

1½ cups buckwheat flour

1 teaspoon kosher salt

½ cup yogurt

4 oz. unsalted butter, softened, plus more as needed

Flaky sea salt, to taste

DIRECTIONS

1. Place the buckwheat flour, kosher salt, yogurt, and butter in a mixing bowl and work the mixture until it comes together as a dough.

2. Place the dough between two sheets of parchment paper and roll it out to about ¼ inch thick. Chill the dough in the refrigerator for 30 minutes.

3. Preheat the oven to 450°F and line two baking sheets with parchment paper. Place some butter in a skillet, melt it over medium heat, and set it aside.

4. Cut the dough into the desired shapes and place the crackers on the baking sheets. Brush each cracker with some of the melted butter and sprinkle the flaky sea salt over them. Place them in the oven and bake until crisp, about 12 minutes. Remove from the oven and let the crackers cool completely before serving.

Margherita Pizza Board

Grilling is a familiar summer activity for many, but, oddly, grilling pizza is not. This board is meant to get your thinking on that turned around, as the char made available by the grill is what you really want in a crust.

A GRILLED PIZZA DOUGH

If you're a sourdough savant, feel free to use that as the leavening agent when preparing the dough.

B PEPPERONI

You might be interested to know that this was not a common pizza topping until the beloved flatbread made its way to America.

C MOZZARELLA CHEESE

Either fior di latte or bufala will work on this board.

D ITALIAN DIPPING OIL

Use the very best balsamic vinegar you can get your hands on in this preparation, aka not the stuff available at a national grocery chain.

E MARINATED MOZZARELLA

If you can't find bocconcini, the miniature balls of mozzarella, simply serve the pesto used to marinate them on the side.

F SLICED TOMATOES

Only the perfectly ripe will suffice on this platter.

Grilled Pizza Dough

YIELD: 4 Servings
ACTIVE TIME: 30 Minutes
TOTAL TIME: 1 Hour and 15 Minutes

INGREDIENTS

2½ teaspoons active dry yeast

1 cup warm water (105°F)

2¾ cups bread flour

2 teaspoons kosher salt

¼ cup extra-virgin olive oil, plus more as needed

DIRECTIONS

1. Place the yeast and water in the work bowl of a stand mixer, gently stir, and let the mixture rest until it starts to foam, about 10 minutes.

2. Add the remaining ingredients, fit the mixer with the dough hook, and work the mixture until it comes together as a smooth dough, about 5 minutes.

3. Coat a mixing bowl with olive oil, place the dough in the bowl, cover it with a kitchen towel, and let the dough rise at room temperature until it has doubled in size, about 45 minutes.

4. Preheat a gas or charcoal grill to 500°F. Preheat the oven to 350°F. Cut the dough into 12 pieces, shape them roughly, and roll them out flat. Brush both sides with olive oil, place them on the grill, and grill until lightly charred on both sides.

5. Place the dough on a baking sheet, place them in the oven, and bake until cooked through and crispy, about 5 minutes. Remove from the oven and serve immediately.

Italian Dipping Oil

YIELD: 1½ Cups
ACTIVE TIME: 5 Minutes
TOTAL TIME: 5 Minutes

INGREDIENTS

1 tablespoon black pepper

2 tablespoons herbs de Provence

1 tablespoon dried thyme

1 tablespoon dried mint

1 tablespoon dried oregano

1 tablespoon garlic powder

3 garlic cloves, minced

1 teaspoon kosher salt

1 teaspoon red pepper flakes

1 cup extra-virgin olive oil

¼ cup balsamic vinegar

DIRECTIONS

1. Combine all of the ingredients, except for the balsamic vinegar, in a mixing bowl and let the mixture sit at room temperature until ready to serve.

2. Stir in the balsamic vinegar right before serving.

Marinated Mozzarella

YIELD: 4 Servings
ACTIVE TIME: 5 Minutes
TOTAL TIME: 5 Minutes

INGREDIENTS

1 (7 oz.) container of miniature balls of mozzarella cheese

Pesto (see page 209)

DIRECTIONS

1. Place the mozzarella and Pesto in a mixing bowl, toss until the cheese is coated, and serve immediately.

Italian Dipping Oil
see page 83

Fiesta Board

The amazing flavors that can be found on the street in Mexico provided the inspiration for this board. Here more than anywhere else in this book, the Grilled Pineapple shows how well fruit can serve as the envoy between the powerful charcuterie kingdoms of meat and cheese.

A SPICY SALAMI

Salumeria Biellese's hot sausage has an upfront, hot sauce–like heat that would be marvelous here.

B GRILLED PINEAPPLE

Don't reserve this preparation for this board, as its mix of sweetness and smoke makes it an ideal summer dessert.

C TEQUILA CHEESE DIP

A show-stopping preparation that delivers on the expectations that will inevitably build as you bring it to the table.

D TORTILLA CHIPS

A hearty chip that can easily break through the melted cheese and withstand the bulk is welcome here.

Grilled Pineapple

YIELD: 4 Servings
ACTIVE TIME: 15 Minutes
TOTAL TIME: 1 Hour

INGREDIENTS

1 pineapple, trimmed and peeled

¼ cup honey

¼ cup brown sugar

½ cup water

Zest and juice of 1 lime

DIRECTIONS

1. Preheat the grill to 450°F. Slice the pineapple into rings that are about ½ inch thick and remove the core.

2. Place the pineapple on the grill and grill until it is charred nicely on both sides, about 6 minutes. Remove from the grill and transfer the pineapple to a baking dish.

3. Combine the honey, brown sugar, water, lime zest, and lime juice in a saucepan and bring it to a boil over medium heat, stirring to dissolve the brown sugar.

4. Pour the syrup over the pineapple and let it marinate for 30 minutes before serving.

Tequila Cheese Dip

YIELD: 4 Servings
ACTIVE TIME: 10 Minutes
TOTAL TIME: 25 Minutes

INGREDIENTS

6 oz. Oaxaca cheese, cubed

½ plum tomato, diced

¼ white onion, diced

2 tablespoons diced green chiles

2 tablespoons sugar

¼ cup fresh lime juice

1 teaspoon chili powder

1 oz. tequila

DIRECTIONS

1. Preheat the oven to 350°F. Place the cheese, tomato, onion, and chiles in a large cast-iron skillet and stir to combine.

2. Combine the sugar, lime juice, and chili powder in a small saucepan and cook over medium heat, stirring to dissolve the sugar, until the mixture is syrupy.

3. Drizzle the syrup over the cheese mixture, place it in the oven, and bake until the cheese has melted and is golden brown on top, about 15 minutes.

4. Remove from the oven, pour the tequila over the top, and use a long match or a wand lighter to ignite it. Bring the flaming skillet to the table and serve once the flames have gone out.

Tequila Cheese Dip

YIELD: 4 Servings
ACTIVE TIME: 10 Minutes
TOTAL TIME: 25 Minutes

INGREDIENTS

6 oz. Oaxaca cheese, cubed

½ plum tomato, diced

¼ white onion, diced

2 tablespoons diced green chiles

2 tablespoons sugar

¼ cup fresh lime juice

1 teaspoon chili powder

1 oz. tequila

DIRECTIONS

1. Preheat the oven to 350°F. Place the cheese, tomato, onion, and chiles in a large cast-iron skillet and stir to combine.

2. Combine the sugar, lime juice, and chili powder in a small saucepan and cook over medium heat, stirring to dissolve the sugar, until the mixture is syrupy.

3. Drizzle the syrup over the cheese mixture, place it in the oven, and bake until the cheese has melted and is golden brown on top, about 15 minutes.

4. Remove from the oven, pour the tequila over the top, and use a long match or a wand lighter to ignite it. Bring the flaming skillet to the table and serve once the flames have gone out.

By the Shore Board

Avocado and crab are a classic pairing once the temperature rises. If you're in the mood to really fashion a memorable board, serve with king crab legs on the side.

A CANDIED RITZ CRACKERS

Improving an already wonderful item is how to lift your boards to legendary heights.

B PICKLED AVOCADO

Adding just a little heat and acid will revolutionize the way you view the avocado forever.

C CRAB DIP

In a pinch, sour cream can be substituted for the crème fraîche here.

D PERSIAN CUCUMBERS

If you're not going to peel them, make sure you wash them very well, perhaps even adding some baking soda to their bath.

Crab Dip

INGREDIENTS

1 tablespoon unsalted butter

½ shallot, minced

¼ cup panko

Salt, to taste

1½ teaspoons dry vermouth

5 oz. cream cheese, softened

¼ cup crème fraîche

¼ cup mayonnaise

1 tablespoon Dijon mustard

¼ cup chopped fresh chives

8 oz. lump crabmeat

½ teaspoon cayenne pepper

½ teaspoon Old Bay seasoning

DIRECTIONS

1. Preheat the oven to 350°F. Place the butter in a skillet and melt it over medium heat. Add the shallot and cook, stirring frequently, until it has softened, about 4 minutes,

2. Stir in the panko and cook until golden brown, 2 to 4 minutes. Remove the pan from heat.

3. Combine the panko mixture and the remaining ingredients in a mixing bowl and then transfer the mixture to a ramekin or a crock. Place the dip in the oven and bake until golden brown on top, about 35 minutes. Remove from the oven and serve immediately.

Pickled Avocado

YIELD: 4 Servings
ACTIVE TIME: 15 Minutes
TOTAL TIME: 5 Hours

INGREDIENTS

1 cup white wine vinegar

1 cup water

⅓ cup sugar

1 tablespoon kosher salt

1 teaspoon red pepper flakes

Flesh of 2 firm avocados

1 garlic clove, smashed

5 sprigs of fresh cilantro

DIRECTIONS

1. Place the vinegar, water, sugar, salt, and red pepper flakes in a medium saucepan and bring to a boil, stirring to dissolve the sugar. Remove the pan from heat and let the brine cool completely.

2. Cut the avocados into wedges and place them in a sterilized mason jar along with the garlic and cilantro. Pour the cooled brine into the jar and let the avocado pickle for at least 4 hours before serving.

Candied Ritz Crackers

YIELD: 4 Servings
ACTIVE TIME: 10 Minutes
TOTAL TIME: 40 Minutes

INGREDIENTS

10 tablespoons unsalted butter

1½ tablespoons brown sugar

6 oz. Ritz crackers

2 teaspoons kosher salt

1 teaspoon garlic powder

1 teaspoon onion powder

¼ teaspoon black pepper

¼ teaspoon red pepper flakes

1 teaspoon Old Bay seasoning

DIRECTIONS

1. Preheat the oven to 350°F and line two baking sheets with parchment paper. Place the butter and brown sugar in a saucepan and melt over medium heat, stirring to combine.

2. Place the crackers in a large mixing bowl, pour the butter mixture over them, and gently stir to combine, taking care not to break the crackers.

3. Place the crackers on the baking sheets and sprinkle some of the remaining ingredients over each one. Place the sheets in the oven and bake until the glaze has hardened, about 12 minutes. Remove and let cool completely before serving.

Fall

As it doesn't encourage excess like the summer does, it is easy to lose sight of the fact that fall is the easiest season to be happy. The brilliance that enters the light, the staggering beauty of the foliage, the exuberance that comes with an unexpected stretch of warm days, and the satisfaction of slipping into a sweater on those nights when a chill first enters the air. These inventive boards are capable of matching these powerful moments, and, at times, improving upon them.

Chicken Curry Board

One of the world's most beloved collection of flavors, the spices that typically feature in a curry, inspired this inventive board.

A CHICKEN SAUSAGE

Making your own sausage is easier than you think, and this preparation will work with any meat you want to swap in for the chicken.

B GOAT CHEESE

Amidst the swirl of bold flavors here, a milder goat cheese will fit in quite nicely.

C SULTANA & MANGO CHUTNEY

Sultanas are golden raisins, made from white seedless grapes.

D CURRIED PISTACHIOS

Pistachios straight-up are wonderful, and when subtly spiced they become heavenly.

E POMEGRANATE REDUCTION

The pop of color this adds is welcome on almost any board, as is concentrating the pomegranate's unique sweet-tart flavor.

F FRIED MUSTARD GREENS

Any greens can be substituted here, but the sharp, peppery taste of mustard greens is a winning choice for this board.

Chicken Sausage

YIELD: 4 Servings
ACTIVE TIME: 30 Minutes
TOTAL TIME: 1 Hour

INGREDIENTS

1 chicken breast, cubed

Salt and pepper, to taste

1 cup heavy cream

¼ cup pistachios, chopped

¼ cup dried apricots, chopped

¼ cup raisins, chopped

DIRECTIONS

1. Season the chicken breast with salt and pepper, place it in a food processor, and blitz for about 5 minutes, until it is a smooth puree.

2. With the food processor running, add the heavy cream in a steady stream and blitz the puree for another 2 minutes.

3. Transfer the chicken puree to a mixing bowl, add the remaining ingredients, and fold until the nuts and fruits are evenly distributed. Divide the mixture into three portions, roll them into logs, and wrap each one in plastic wrap as tightly as possible. Tie the ends with kitchen twine and poke a few small holes in the logs with a needle.

4. Prepare an ice bath. Bring water to a strong simmer in a medium saucepan, making sure it does not come to a boil. Place the logs, keeping them in the plastic wrap, in the pan and poach until their internal temperature reaches 165°F, about 15 minutes.

5. Remove the sausages from the water and submerge them in the ice bath until completely cool. Chill in the refrigerator until ready to serve.

Curried Pistachios

YIELD: 4 Servings
ACTIVE TIME: 10 Minutes
TOTAL TIME: 30 Minutes

INGREDIENTS

1 cup unshelled roasted pistachios

½ cup shelled roasted pistachios

½ teaspoon curry powder

1 tablespoon extra-virgin olive oil

½ teaspoon fine sea salt

DIRECTIONS

1. Preheat the oven to 350°F. Place the pistachios in a mixing bowl, add the remaining ingredients, and toss until the nuts are coated.

2. Place the nuts on a baking sheet, place them in the oven, and roast until fragrant, about 12 minutes. Remove from the oven and let the pistachios cool before serving.

Sultana & Mango Chutney

YIELD: 1 Cup
ACTIVE TIME: 10 Minutes
TOTAL TIME: 20 Minutes

INGREDIENTS

1½ tablespoons extra-virgin olive oil

½ red onion, diced

½ teaspoon red pepper flakes

½ teaspoon curry powder

½ teaspoon grated fresh ginger

1 garlic clove, minced

⅓ cup red wine vinegar

½ cup mango jam

¼ cup sultanas (golden raisins)

⅓ cup water

DIRECTIONS

1. Place the olive oil in a large skillet and warm it over medium heat. When the oil starts to shimmer, add the onion, red pepper flakes, and curry powder and cook, stirring frequently, until the onion starts to soften, about 3 minutes.

2. Stir in the ginger and garlic, cook for 1 minute, and then add the remaining ingredients. Bring to a simmer and cook until the mixture has reduced. Transfer to a serving dish and serve warm or at room temperature.

Pomegranate Reduction

YIELD: ½ Cup
ACTIVE TIME: 10 Minutes
TOTAL TIME: 10 Minutes

INGREDIENTS

8 oz. pomegranate juice

DIRECTIONS

1. Place the juice in a saucepan and cook over medium heat until it is thick enough to coat the back of a wooden spoon. Remove from heat and let cool before serving.

Fried Mustard Greens

YIELD: 4 Servings
ACTIVE TIME: 20 Minutes
TOTAL TIME: 30 Minutes

INGREDIENTS

1 bunch of mustard greens

4 cups canola oil

Salt, to taste

DIRECTIONS

1. Remove the mustard green leaves from their stems and rinse them well. Pat them dry with paper towels and set them aside.

2. Place the canola oil in a wide and deep cast-iron skillet and warm it to 300°F over medium heat. Add the greens and fry, turning them over once, until crispy, 1 to 2 minutes. Remove with a slotted spoon, place them on a paper towel–lined plate to drain, and season with salt. Serve once they have cooled slightly.

Camembert & Maple Board

If you haven't tried a warmed Camembert beside the fire on an early autumn night, prepare this board immediately.

 PROSCIUTTO

A nice pancetta or a few slices of crisped-up bacon will also agree with this board.

B **BAKED CAMEMBERT**

The provided instructions are for the oven, but if you find yourself fireside with a cast-iron skillet in tow, don't hesitate to prepare it there.

 APPLES

Slice them into wedges for dipping into the Camembert, and matchsticks for wrapping in the prosciutto.

D **PUMPERNICKEL BREAD**

Toasted or untoasted, both will be wonderful with the other elements of the board.

Baked Camembert

YIELD: 4 Servings
ACTIVE TIME: 5 Minutes
TOTAL TIME: 25 Minutes

INGREDIENTS

1 wheel of Camembert cheese

1 cup Granola (see page 121)

½ cup maple syrup

DIRECTIONS

1. Preheat the oven to 350°F. Place the Camembert in a small cast-iron skillet. Sprinkle the Granola over the cheese and drizzle the maple syrup on top.

2. Place in the oven and bake until the cheese has softened, about 10 minutes. Remove from the oven and serve immediately.

YIELD: 3 Cups
ACTIVE TIME: 10 Minutes
TOTAL TIME: 45 Minutes

Granola

INGREDIENTS

2 cups rolled oats

¼ cup maple syrup

1 cup pecan halves

2 teaspoons kosher salt

1 teaspoon cinnamon

⅔ cup dried cranberries

DIRECTIONS

1. Preheat the oven to 350°F and line a baking sheet with a silpat mat. Place all of the ingredients in a mixing bowl and toss to combine.

2. Spread the mixture on the baking sheet in an even layer. Place it in the oven and bake until browned and fragrant, about 20 minutes. Remove from the oven and let the granola cool completely before serving.

Fall Harvest Board

The fall harvest is about celebrating the incredible bounty the natural world has provided, and the considerable labor put in by those charged with cultivating it. This vegan board takes that spirit and runs with it.

A VEGAN SAUSAGE

For this and the roast loaf, Sweet Earth and Field Roast are good options to look for.

B VEGAN ROAST LOAF

Those interested in veering away from the vegan direction of this board would do well with smoked turkey breast or a honeyed ham.

C HARD CASHEW CHEESE

Fans of this creamy nut will not be surprised by the revelation of its effectiveness as a base for making cheese.

D SOFT CASHEW CHEESE

This is actually manageable to make at home. If you're intrigued, take a gander at some of the recipes available online.

E ESCABECHE

A spicy mélange of pickled vegetables. The provided preparation is traditional-leaning, meaning you shouldn't hesitate to swap in whatever vegetables you want.

F RASPBERRY & CHIA JAM

Fresh or frozen raspberries can be used to make this jam.

G CHIA SEED CRACKERS

Rich in nutrients and omega-3s, chia seeds are also dazzling when studding these gluten-free crackers.

Escabeche

INGREDIENTS

1 carrot, peeled and sliced

1 cup cauliflower florets

1 radish, sliced thin

6 green beans, chopped

½ jalapeño pepper, sliced thin

2 garlic cloves, smashed

1½ teaspoons sugar

½ teaspoon fine sea salt

½ teaspoon peppercorns

½ cup distilled white vinegar

1 cup water

DIRECTIONS

1. Layer the vegetables in a sterilized mason jar.

2. Place the remaining ingredients in a saucepan and bring to a boil over medium-high heat, stirring to dissolve the sugar. Pour the brine over the vegetables and let the mixture cool to room temperature. Cover the jar and chill it in the refrigerator for at least 4 hours before serving.

Raspberry & Chia Jam

YIELD: 2 Cups
ACTIVE TIME: 20 Minutes
TOTAL TIME: 1 Hour and 30 Minutes

INGREDIENTS

2 cups raspberries

2 tablespoons water

1 tablespoon fresh lemon juice

3 tablespoons chia seeds

3 tablespoons honey

DIRECTIONS

1. Place the raspberries and water in a saucepan and cook over medium heat for 2 minutes.

2. Stir in the remaining ingredients and cook until the mixture has thickened and acquired a jammy consistency. Remove from heat and let the jam cool completely before serving.

Chia Seed Crackers

YIELD: 30 Crackers
ACTIVE TIME: 20 Minutes
TOTAL TIME: 2 Hours

INGREDIENTS

9 tablespoons chia seeds

5 tablespoons water

½ cup almond flour

½ teaspoon kosher salt

¼ teaspoon black pepper

DIRECTIONS

1. Use a spice grinder or a mortar and pestle to grind 1 tablespoon of the chia seeds into a powder. Transfer the powder to a bowl and add 3 tablespoons of the water. Gently stir to combine and let the mixture rest for 10 minutes.

2. Add the remaining chia seeds and water along with the almond flour, salt, and pepper. Fold until the mixture comes together as a dough, place it between two sheets of parchment paper, and roll out until it is approximately ¼ inch thick. Chill the dough in the refrigerator for 30 minutes.

3. Preheat the oven to 350°F and line two baking sheets with parchment paper. Cut the dough into the desired shapes and place them on the baking sheets. Place them in the oven and bake until the crackers are golden brown, about 20 minutes. Remove from the oven and let the crackers cool completely.

Black & Blue Board

Anyone who has enjoyed a Martini garnished with blue cheese olives, a dry-aged steak, and a side of sautéed mushrooms at a fine steakhouse will recognize the genius of this board straight off.

A BEEF TATAKI

A Japanese preparation that features their knack for bringing out the best of an ingredient.

B POINT REYES BLUE CHEESE

Try to arrange as many bites as you can that combine the creaminess of this cheese and the acid of the pickled onion.

C PICKLED RED ONION

Another offering that's always good to have on hand, as it makes for a wonderful topping for tacos, salads, fried rice, and many more dishes.

D DUXELLES

A finely chopped mixture of sautéed mushrooms, onions or shallots, and herbs (parsley is traditional, I prefer thyme) that can be enjoyed as is, as a stuffing, or used as the base for a simple, flavorful sauce.

YIELD: 4 Servings

ACTIVE TIME: 20 Minutes

TOTAL TIME: 1 Hour and 30 Minutes

Beef Tataki

INGREDIENTS

8 oz. beef tenderloin

Salt and pepper, to taste

1 tablespoon extra-virgin olive oil, plus more as needed

Juice of 1 orange

2 garlic cloves, minced

1 teaspoon sugar

1 teaspoon grated fresh ginger

1 teaspoon Dijon mustard

DIRECTIONS

1. Cut the tenderloin in half and tie each piece with kitchen twine so that it will maintain its shape while being seared. Season the tenderloin with salt and pepper.

2. Coat the bottom of a large skillet with olive oil and warm it over medium-high heat. When the oil starts to shimmer, place the pieces of tenderloin in the pan and cook, turning them as they brown. Remove the tenderloins from the pan and let cool to room temperature.

3. Place the remaining ingredients in a bowl and stir to combine. Add the tenderloins and let them marinate for at least 1 hour before serving.

Duxelles

INGREDIENTS

1 tablespoon extra-virgin olive oil

3 portobello mushrooms, finely diced

½ shallot, minced

2 tablespoons fresh thyme, chopped

Salt and pepper, to taste

DIRECTIONS

1. Place the olive oil in a large skillet and warm it over medium heat. When the oil starts to shimmer, add the mushrooms and cook, stirring frequently, until they have released all of their liquid, about 8 minutes.

2. Stir in the shallot and thyme, cook, stirring occasionally, for 2 minutes, and transfer the mixture to a food processor. Pulse until the desired texture has been achieved.

3. Season with salt and pepper and serve.

Pickled Red Onion

YIELD: 4 Servings

ACTIVE TIME: 15 Minutes

TOTAL TIME: 5 Hours

INGREDIENTS

1 red onion, sliced thin

1 tablespoon black peppercorns

Pinch of kosher salt

1 cup red wine

1 cup red wine vinegar

1 cup sugar

DIRECTIONS

1. Place the onion, peppercorns, and salt in a sterilized mason jar.

2. Combine the wine, vinegar, and sugar in a saucepan and bring the mixture to a boil, stirring to dissolve the sugar.

3. Pour the brine into the mason jar and let it come to room temperature before placing the pickled onion in the refrigerator. Chill for at least 4 hours before serving.

Duxelles
see page 133

Pecan & Prune Board

Not a classic combination—yet. This board was a delicious bit of serendipity inspired by a simple play on words: prune a pecan tree.

A GRAPES

Red, green, or Concord will all work well on this board.

B SALAMI

Consider branching out and going with Olympic Provisions' Loukanika, which hails from Oregon, as its combination of sweetness and spice is unique in the cured meat universe.

C CAPOCOLLO

You may know it as "gabagool," which is its translation in the Napolitan dialect that many Italian Americans use.

D STUFFED PRUNES

Green Island blue cheese, a Danish offering that thrives when partnered with something sweet, is your best bet for this preparation.

E PECAN & BLUE CHEESE CRACKERS

The key here is the 24-hour rest period. If you cut that short, your crackers will separate in the oven and melt.

Stuffed Prunes

YIELD: 4 Servings
ACTIVE TIME: 10 Minutes
TOTAL TIME: 10 Minutes

INGREDIENTS

15 dried prunes

3 oz. blue cheese, crumbled

DIRECTIONS

1. Cut a slit in the top of each prune, stuff them with the blue cheese, and either serve immediately or chill in the refrigerator. If refrigerating, let the stuffed prunes come to room temperature before serving.

Pecan & Blue Cheese Crackers

YIELD: 30 Crackers
ACTIVE TIME: 20 Minutes
TOTAL TIME: 25 Hours

INGREDIENTS

¾ cup pecans

¾ cup all-purpose flour

4 tablespoons unsalted butter, grated

3 oz. blue cheese

1 tablespoon fresh thyme, chopped

1 teaspoon kosher salt

DIRECTIONS

1. Place all of the ingredients in a food processor and pulse until the mixture comes together as a dough.

2. Place the dough between two sheets of parchment paper and roll it out until it is about ¼ inch thick. Place the dough in the refrigerator and chill for 24 hours.

3. Preheat the oven to 350°F and line two baking sheets with parchment paper. Cut the crackers into the desired shapes, place them on the baking sheets, and bake in the oven until crispy, about 15 minutes. Remove from the oven and let cool before serving.

Pecan & Blue
Cheese Crackers
see page 141

Winter

Between the dwindling light, plunging temperatures, and holiday-driven demands on one's time, the winter can be a bear. All of these antagonisms only mean one thing to the gifted entertainer: it's time to shine, and bring people together. With a series of boards that range from classy to comforting, we'll help you keep spirits high.

Up in Smoke Board

Derek's background in fine dining trained him to have a Pavlovian reaction every time he sees a glass cloche: cheese and smoke. It is not just for show—though it is quite a spectacle—the piney scent of the torched rosemary will have a marked effect on the cheese.

 TUSCAN SALAMI

Finocchina, a salami flavored with fennel seeds, is a strong selection for this board.

B **CYPRESS GROVE HUMBOLDT FOG CHEESE**

With a vein of edible ash running through it, this creamy, complex cheese feels as though it was conceived in a dream, mainly because it was.

C **POACHED PEARS**

Don't hesitate to experiment with the spices you add to the poaching liquid.

D **BLACK PEPPER LAVASH**

A thin flatbread that will be right at home beside the cheese and rosemary, thanks to the infusion of black pepper.

E **SMOKED ROSEMARY**

This is so easy there's no need to compose a separate preparation for it. Simply ignite four to five sprigs, shake them until the flames are extinguished, place them on a board, place the cheese on top, and cover with a cloche.

Poached Pears

YIELD: 2 Servings
ACTIVE TIME: 10 Minutes
TOTAL TIME: 30 Minutes

INGREDIENTS

1 cinnamon stick

2 star anise pods

1 cup water

1 cup red wine

½ cup sugar

2 Anjou pears, peeled and cored

Peel of ½ orange

DIRECTIONS

1. Place all of the ingredients, except for the pears and orange peel, in a saucepan and bring to a simmer.

2. Slice each pear into eight wedges and add them to the pan along with the orange peel. Reduce heat to medium-low and cook until pears have softened, about 15 minutes. Remove the pears with a strainer and serve immediately.

Black Pepper Lavash

YIELD: 1 Flatbread
ACTIVE TIME: 15 Minutes
TOTAL TIME: 1 Hour

INGREDIENTS

2½ cups all-purpose flour

2 teaspoons kosher salt

1 teaspoon sugar

⅔ cup warm water (105°F)

1 egg

3 tablespoons unsalted butter, melted

Freshly cracked black pepper, to taste

DIRECTIONS

1. Place the flour, salt, and sugar in a mixing bowl and stir to combine. Add the warm water and work the mixture by hand until it has been incorporated. Add the egg and knead the mixture until it comes together as a smooth dough. Cover the bowl with plastic wrap and let the dough rest at room temperature for 30 minutes.

2. Preheat the oven to 375°F. Brush a baking sheet with some of the butter. Place the dough on the baking sheet and roll it out until it is as thin as possible. Brush the dough with the remaining butter and generously season it with the cracked black pepper.

3. Place the flatbread in the oven and bake until it is golden brown, 15 to 20 minutes. Remove from the oven and let the lavash cool slightly before serving.

Black Pepper Lavash
see page 151

Honey & Bourbon Board

On its face, this board seems to be all about sweetness—but the inclusion of the extremely savory duck prosciutto and the creamy gouda provide the proper balance.

 DUCK PROSCIUTTO

A specialty item that you should absolutely add to your charcuterie rotation. If intrigued, head to D'Artagnan's specialty online food store.

 BOURBON GOUDA CHEESE

A more traditional gouda will also serve you well here.

 CHOCOLATE CHERRY CRACKERS

You can also enjoy these with tea, or for dessert.

 HONEYCOMB CANDY

A very simple entry into candy making, and good enough to propel you onward into more involved preparations.

 AMERICAN WHISKEY

Not essential, but a glass of either bourbon or rye on the rocks will be wonderful with this board.

Chocolate Cherry Crackers

YIELD: 30 Crackers
ACTIVE TIME: 15 Minutes
TOTAL TIME: 1 Hour and 30 Minutes

INGREDIENTS

½ cup all-purpose flour

½ cup wheat flour

¼ cup brown sugar

¼ cup cocoa powder

½ teaspoon fine sea salt

4 oz. unsalted butter, cold and cubed

3 tablespoons whole milk

½ cup dried cherries

⅓ cup sunflower seeds

DIRECTIONS

1. Place all of the ingredients in a food processor and pulse until the mixture comes together as a dough.

2. Place the dough between two sheets of parchment paper and roll out until it is ¼ inch thick. Place the dough in the refrigerator and chill for 45 minutes.

3. Preheat the oven to 350°F and line two baking sheets with parchment paper. Cut the dough into the desired shapes, place them on the baking sheets, and bake in the oven until crisp, about 12 minutes. Remove and let cool completely before serving.

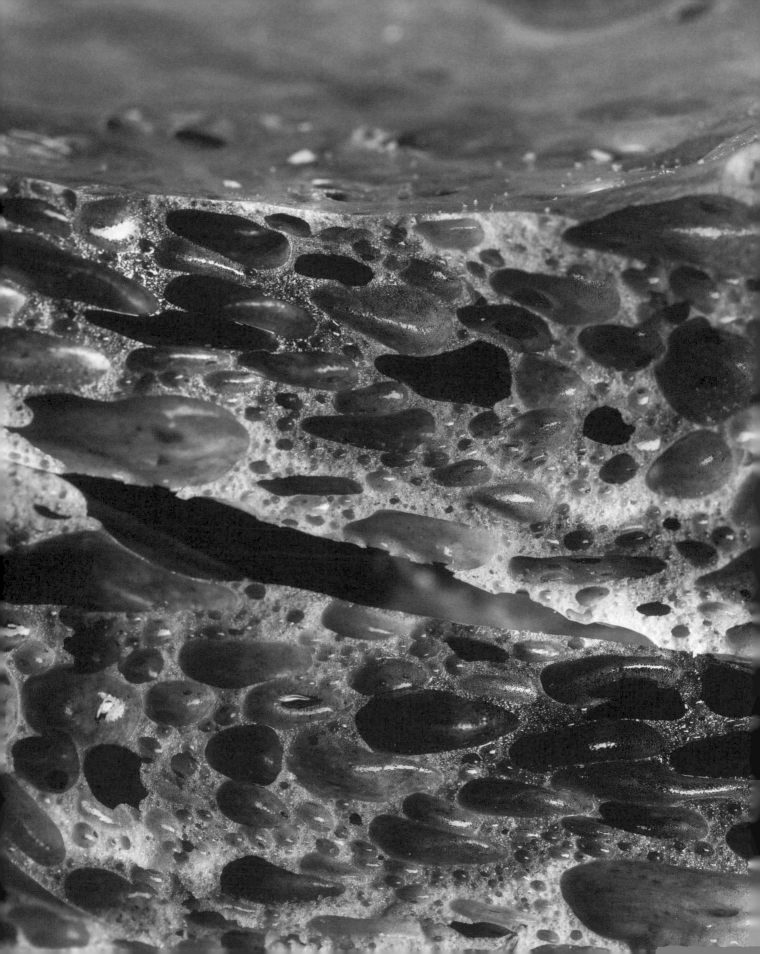

Honeycomb Candy

YIELD: 4 Servings
ACTIVE TIME: 15 Minutes
TOTAL TIME: 1 Hour

INGREDIENTS

1 cup sugar

¼ cup light corn syrup

2 tablespoons honey

½ cup water

2 teaspoons baking soda

DIRECTIONS

1. Line a square, 8-inch baking dish with parchment paper. Place the sugar, corn syrup, honey, and water in a medium saucepan fitted with a candy thermometer and cook over medium heat, stirring occasionally, until the mixture comes to a boil. Continue to cook, without stirring, until the mixture is 300°F and has turned light amber in color.

2. Remove from heat and carefully and quickly stir in the baking soda. Pour the mixture into the baking dish, place it in the refrigerator, and chill for at least 45 minutes.

3. Break the mixture into bite-sized pieces and serve.

Chocolate Cherry Crackers see page 156

Game Board

An arrangement meant to celebrate the deer's life, from the far-ranging diet it enjoys while roaming over the land to the very end, when it blesses us with the gift of its uniquely delicious meat.

Ⓐ VENISON TARTARE

For those who are anxious about the thought of raw meat: when basic rules of sanitary food prep are followed and fresh meat is used, the risk is minimal.

Ⓑ VENISON JERKY

Those of you who have a smoker may want to consider making the jerky in there, rather than in a food dehydrator.

Ⓒ GOUDA CHEESE

The strong, complex finish provided by Boerenkaas' offering is an exceptional choice here.

Ⓓ PEPPERCORN ASIAGO CHEESE

Pairing the nutty nature of Asiago with a bit of spice makes this offering an autumn standby.

Ⓔ CRANBERRY RELISH

A bite consisting of this and the venison jerky is a small piece of paradise.

Ⓕ GINGERBREAD

After a few soft, pillowy slices of this, you'll never go back to the rock-hard gingerbread men that reign around the holidays.

Ⓖ ORANGE MARMALADE

A marmalade is a preserve made from the juice and peels of citrus, and traditionally, it features bitter oranges, such as the Seville. Blood oranges also work well as a marmalade.

Venison Tartare

YIELD: 4 Servings
ACTIVE TIME: 10 Minutes
TOTAL TIME: 10 Minutes

INGREDIENTS

1 cup diced venison loin

2 tablespoons minced shallot

1 tablespoon mayonnaise

1 teaspoon Dijon mustard

2 tablespoons chopped fresh parsley

Salt and pepper, to taste

DIRECTIONS

1. Place all of the ingredients in a bowl, taste the mixture, and adjust the seasoning as needed.

2. Use a mold to form it into a tower and serve immediately.

Venison Jerky

YIELD: 4 Servings
ACTIVE TIME: 15 Minutes
TOTAL TIME: 7 to 9 Hours

INGREDIENTS

8 oz. venison tri-tip, sliced thin

1 tablespoon soy sauce

1 teaspoon distilled white vinegar

1 teaspoon sesame oil

½ teaspoon honey

¼ teaspoon onion powder

¼ teaspoon minced garlic

⅛ teaspoon grated fresh ginger

DIRECTIONS

1. Place all of the ingredients in a mixing bowl and stir to combine. Let the venison marinate for 1 hour.

2. Place the venison on parchment-lined baking sheets, place them in a food dehydrator, and dehydrate at 140°F for 6 to 8 hours. When it is ready, the jerky should have lost about one-third of its weight and have a slightly bouncy texture.

Cranberry Relish

YIELD: 2 Cups

ACTIVE TIME: 5 Minutes

TOTAL TIME: 1 Hour

INGREDIENTS

12 oz. cranberries

1 Granny Smith apple, cored and diced

Segments of ½ orange

1 cup sugar

DIRECTIONS

1. Place the cranberries in a food processor and pulse for 1 minute. Add the apple and orange and pulse until combined. Add the sugar and pulse until incorporated.

2. Transfer the mixture to a bowl and let it macerate for at least 1 hour before serving.

YIELD: 4 Servings
ACTIVE TIME: 20 Minutes
TOTAL TIME: 1 Hour and 15 Minutes

Gingerbread

INGREDIENTS

1½ cups all-purpose flour

1 teaspoon baking soda

½ teaspoon kosher salt

2 teaspoons ground ginger

1 teaspoon cinnamon

¼ teaspoon ground cloves

2 oz. unsalted butter, melted

⅔ cup dark brown sugar

⅔ cup molasses

⅔ cup boiling water

1 egg

Confectioners' sugar, for dusting

DIRECTIONS

1. Preheat the oven to 350°F and coat a square, 8-inch baking dish with nonstick cooking spray. Place the flour, baking soda, salt, ginger, cinnamon, and cloves in a mixing bowl and whisk to combine.

2. Place the butter, brown sugar, molasses, and water in a separate bowl and whisk to combine. Add the egg, whisk to incorporate, and then add the dry mixture. Fold until the mixture comes together as a smooth batter and pour it into the baking dish.

3. Bake in the oven until a cake tester inserted into the center comes out clean, about 35 minutes. Remove from the oven and let cool for 20 minutes before dusting with the confectioners' sugar, slicing, and serving.

Orange Marmalade

YIELD: 2 Cups

ACTIVE TIME: 30 Minutes

TOTAL TIME: 4 Hours

INGREDIENTS

2 oranges, sliced

2 lemons, sliced

4 cups water

4 cups sugar

DIRECTIONS

1. Place all of the ingredients in a large saucepan fitted with a candy thermometer. Cook over medium-low heat, stirring occasionally, until the mixture reaches 220°F, about 2 hours.

2. Pour the marmalade into a mason jar and let it cool completely before serving or storing in the refrigerator.

Orange Marmalade
see page 172

Bagel Board

Though it is difficult to outshine a good bagel, we believe the Cured Egg Yolks pull it off—each one bringing to mind the glory of the morning sun, and a versatile preparation that can easily share its richness with an uncountable number of dishes. Start here with them, move onto salads and pasta dishes, and then keep going until you hit your limit.

A **BEET-CURED SALMON**

The sweet, earthy flavor of the beets is beautiful beside the mild, refreshing flavor of salmon.

B **PICKLED FENNEL**

Adding a few pinches of red pepper flakes to the brine is worth considering if you like things spicy.

C **CAPER CREAM CHEESE**

Spiking the mild flavor of cream cheese with the piquant taste of capers is the type of simple, significant improvement that can revolutionize your work in the kitchen.

D **BAGEL CHIPS**

It is difficult to better a good bagel, but these crispy thins manage the task.

E **CURED EGG YOLKS**

Beautiful, and slightly alien looking, these will draw everyone in with their looks, and please with their rich taste.

F **CHARRED LEMON**

The juice of these will also be wonderful squeezed over a salad or a fillet of whitefish.

Beet-Cured Salmon

YIELD: 4 Servings
ACTIVE TIME: 30 Minutes
TOTAL TIME: 16 Hours

INGREDIENTS

2 cups chopped beets

1 cup kosher salt

½ cup sugar

1 cup water

1 lb. salmon, skinned and boned

DIRECTIONS

1. Place the beets, salt, and sugar in a food processor and pulse until the beets are finely chopped. Add the water in a slow stream and pulse until the mixture is a smooth puree.

2. Place the salmon in a baking dish and pour the puree over it. Place the salmon in the refrigerator and let it cure for at least 12 hours.

3. Rinse the salmon under cold water. Place it on a wire rack set in a rimmed baking sheet and let it dry, uncovered, in the refrigerator for 4 hours before serving.

Cured Egg Yolks

YIELD: 4 Servings
ACTIVE TIME: 30 Minutes
TOTAL TIME: 3 Days

INGREDIENTS

1½ cups kosher salt

½ cup sugar

4 egg yolks

DIRECTIONS

1. Combine the salt and sugar in wide bowl. Using a spoon, create four shallow wells in the mixture, one for each yolk.

2. Carefully place each yolk into its own well. Spoon the mixture over the yolks until they are covered completely.

3. Cover the bowl with plastic wrap, place it in the refrigerator, and let the egg yolks cure for 3 days.

4. Remove the yolks from the mixture, rinse under cold water, and slice before serving.

Bagel Chips

INGREDIENTS

3 everything bagels, sliced thin

DIRECTIONS

1. Preheat the oven to 350°F.

2. Place the bagel slices on baking sheets and toast them in the oven until crispy and golden brown, about 8 minutes. Remove from the oven and let the chips cool slightly before serving.

Pickled Fennel

YIELD: 4 Servings
ACTIVE TIME: 20 Minutes
TOTAL TIME: 8 Hours

INGREDIENTS

1 bulb of fennel, trimmed and sliced

2 fennel fronds

1 teaspoon kosher salt

1 teaspoon mustard seeds

½ teaspoon fennel seeds

1 cup water

1 cup sugar

1 cup white wine vinegar

DIRECTIONS

1. Place fennel, fronds, salt, mustard seeds, and fennel seeds in a sterilized mason jar.

2. Place the water, sugar, and vinegar in a saucepan and bring it to a boil, stirring to dissolve the sugar. Pour the brine over the fennel and let it cool to room temperature.

3. Place in the refrigerator and chill for at least 6 hours before serving.

Charred Lemon

YIELD: 4 Servings
ACTIVE TIME: 5 Minutes
TOTAL TIME: 15 Minutes

INGREDIENTS

1 lemon, halved

DIRECTIONS

1. Warm a dry cast-iron skillet over medium heat.

2. When the pan is hot, place the lemon in it, cut side down, and sear until charred and caramelized, about 5 minutes. Squeeze the juice over the salmon or slice extremely thin to serve.

Caper Cream Cheese

YIELD: 4 Servings
ACTIVE TIME: 5 Minutes
TOTAL TIME: 5 Minutes

INGREDIENTS

8 oz. cream cheese, softened

3 tablespoons capers, drained and rinsed

DIRECTIONS

1. Place the cream cheese in a bowl, add the capers, and fold until they are evenly distributed. Serve immediately.

Hunter's Board

The preservation of game meats sustained many a people throughout history. Refrigeration has done away with the need to rely on it, but when you're enjoying this board you'll see that those gains in convenience have cost us something in taste.

A WILD BOAR LONZA

Another specialty item that you will want to turn to D'Artagnan for. A tip: you want to keep the fat on, as it adds considerably to the flavor.

B DUCK RILLETTE

A simple spread with a flavor so rewarding that you may actually feel a slight guilt creeping in.

C COMTÉ CHEESE

A French cheese that will change considerably as it ages, growing fruity, spicy, and nutty.

D VERMONT CREAMERY BIJOU CHEESE

This is wondrous beside the richness of the rillette and savory lonza.

E RED LENTIL CRACKERS

Turning lentils into a flour opens many doors for the creative cook. These crackers lie behind one.

F CINNAMON MUSTARD

Cinnamon's brightness bolsters the already strong flavor of Dijon mustard.

G BOYSENBERRY JAM

As sweet and floral as raspberry, but with a bit more sourness, a boysenberry-based preserve is the best bet here.

Duck Rillette

YIELD: 4 Servings
ACTIVE TIME: 15 Minutes
TOTAL TIME: 1 Hour

INGREDIENTS

1 duck leg, confit (see below)

2 tablespoons duck fat

2 tablespoons chopped fresh parsley

Salt and pepper, to taste

1 tablespoon unsalted butter, melted and cooled

DIRECTIONS

1. Remove the meat from the duck leg and finely chop it. Place the meat in a mixing bowl.

2. Add the duck fat and parsley, fold to combine, and season the mixture with salt and pepper.

3. Place the mixture in a small jar, top it with the melted butter, and refrigerate until ready to serve. The rillette will keep in the refrigerator for 5 to 7 days.

Duck Confit

To make a confit of duck legs, pat 6 duck legs dry with paper towels and season them generously with salt. With the tip of a knife, gently poke the skin all around each leg. This will help release the fat as it renders. Let the legs rest at room temperature for at least 25 minutes. Coat the bottom of a Dutch oven with the olive oil, add the duck legs, and set the oven to 285°F. Place the Dutch oven, uncovered, in the oven. You do not want to preheat the oven, as starting the duck at a low temperature allows its fat to render. After 1½ hours, check the duck. It should be under a layer of duck fat and the skin should be getting crisp. If the legs aren't browned and crispy, let the duck cook longer. When the skin is starting to crisp, raise the oven's temperature to 375°F and cook the duck for another 15 minutes. Remove the pot from the oven, remove the duck legs from the fat, and let them rest for 10 minutes before using as desired.

Red Lentil Crackers

YIELD: 15 Crackers
ACTIVE TIME: 20 Minutes
TOTAL TIME: 1 Hour and 45 Minutes

INGREDIENTS

1 cup red lentils

½ cup water

1 teaspoon fine sea salt, plus more to taste

Canola oil, as needed

DIRECTIONS

1. Place the lentils in a food processor and pulse until finely ground. Add the water in a slow stream and pulse until the mixture comes together as a dough. Add the salt and pulse until incorporated.

2. Coat two pieces of parchment paper with nonstick cooking spray. Place the dough between the pieces of parchment and roll it out until ½ inch thick. Place in the refrigerator and chill for 1 hour.

3. Add canola oil to a Dutch oven until it is about 2 inches deep and warm it to 350°F over medium heat.

4. Cut the dough into rounds, add them to the oil, and fry until puffy and crisp, about 5 minutes. Transfer to a paper towel–lined plate, season with salt, and let the crackers cool completely before serving.

Cinnamon Mustard

YIELD: 4 Servings
ACTIVE TIME: 5 Minutes
TOTAL TIME: 5 Minutes

INGREDIENTS

¼ cup Dijon mustard

½ teaspoon cinnamon,
plus more to taste

DIRECTIONS

1. Combine the ingredients in a ramekin and sprinkle more cinnamon on top before serving.

Pub Board

The perfect board for a Sunday filled with nothing but food, football, and friends.

A BRATWURST

This famed German is no doubt familiar. To really lean into the pub theme, poach them in beer, butter, and onions before searing.

B SOFT PRETZELS

Should you go with the bites, these are particularly easy. However, committing to the full-fledged classic is worth the investment of time and energy.

C BEER CHEESE

The richer the brown ale you use, the better this dip will be.

D DARK BEER

Any stout or brown ale will be best here. But, of course, the ubiquitous IPA will also work.

E CORNICHONS

The miniature gherkin cucumbers whose acidic bite will be welcome beside the cheddar, Beer Cheese, and pretzels.

F SPICY MUSTARD

Go with the liveliest version you can handle, as the pretzels will improve as the temperature in your mouth rises.

Soft Pretzels

YIELD: 4 Servings
ACTIVE TIME: 45 Minutes
TOTAL TIME: 2 Hours

INGREDIENTS

½ cup warm water (105°F)

2 tablespoons brown sugar

¼ teaspoon instant yeast

6 tablespoons unsalted butter, melted

2½ teaspoons fine sea salt

4½ cups all-purpose flour

⅓ cup baking soda

1 egg

1 tablespoon room-temperature water

Coarse sea salt, to taste

DIRECTIONS

1. In the work bowl of a stand mixer fitted with the dough hook, combine the warm water, brown sugar, yeast, and melted butter and beat on low for 5 minutes.

2. Add the fine sea salt and flour, raise the speed to medium, and knead for 4 minutes. Coat a large mixing bowl with nonstick cooking spray, transfer the dough to the bowl, and cover it with plastic wrap. Let the dough rest at room temperature until it has doubled in size, about 1 hour.

3. Cut the dough into ½-inch-thick ropes. Cut the ropes into bites or twist them into traditional pretzel shapes.

4. Preheat the oven to 425°F. Line two baking sheets with parchment paper and coat with nonstick cooking spray. Bring water to a boil in a medium saucepan. Gradually add the baking soda and gently stir to combine.

5. Place the pretzels in the water and poach them briefly—30 seconds for bites, 1 minute for traditional pretzels. Carefully remove the pretzels with a slotted spoon and transfer them to the baking sheets.

6. Place the 1 egg and room-temperature water in a small bowl, beat to combine, and brush the egg wash over the pretzels. Sprinkle the coarse sea salt over the pretzels and bake them in the oven until golden brown, about 15 minutes. Remove from the oven and briefly let cool before serving.

Beer Cheese

YIELD: 4 Servings
ACTIVE TIME: 20 Minutes
TOTAL TIME: 20 Minutes

INGREDIENTS

2 tablespoons unsalted butter

1½ teaspoons all-purpose flour

¾ cup brown ale

1 tablespoon Worcestershire sauce

½ teaspoon mustard powder

Pinch of cayenne pepper

1½ cups grated cheddar cheese

Salt and pepper, to taste

DIRECTIONS

1. Place the butter in a saucepan and melt it over medium heat. Add the flour and stir constantly until the mixture starts to brown, about 2 minutes.

2. Deglaze the pan with the brown ale and Worcestershire sauce, scraping up any browned bits from the bottom of the pan.

3. Add the remaining ingredients, cook until the cheese has melted, and serve immediately.

YIELD: 4 Servings
ACTIVE TIME: 10 Minutes
TOTAL TIME: 20 Minutes

Bratwurst

INGREDIENTS

Extra-virgin olive oil, as needed

4 bratwurst

DIRECTIONS

1. Coat the bottom of a large skillet with olive oil and warm it over medium heat.

2. Place the bratwurst in the pan and cook, turning occasionally, until their internal temperature is 145°F.

Soft Pretzels
see page 198

Antipasto Board

This board does not necessarily need to be slotted as a winter-only board. With all the entertaining that goes on around the holidays though, and the appreciation it tends to meet with, it's a safe place to be able to turn when the stress of the season starts to grate.

A **SALAMI**

Tuscan, Italian Dry, and Secchi are the trio shown here, but feel free to insert your own favorites.

B **FONTINA CHEESE**

A gentle, semisoft cheese with a taste that is both buttery and nutty. It's also extremely good on a grilled cheese in place of the cheddar.

C **TAPENADE**

The recipe recommends the widely available Kalamata, but any olive at all can be used in this spread.

D **ARUGULA**

The peppery bite is a nice counter to the trio of salty cured meats.

E **PESTO**

If you'd like this to have a little more texture, and you're in need of an arm workout, make this with a mortar and pestle.

F **CRUSTY BREAD**

If you can't get to your favorite bakery in time to snag a loaf, toast a less-than-artisan offering in the oven or on the grill to cover your tracks.

YIELD: ½ Cup
ACTIVE TIME: 10 Minutes
TOTAL TIME: 10 Minutes

Tapenade

INGREDIENTS

½ cup finely chopped Kalamata olives

1 teaspoon capers, drained, rinsed, and finely chopped

1 teaspoon finely chopped sun-dried tomatoes in olive oil

1 teaspoon dried oregano

DIRECTIONS

1. Combine all of the ingredients in a mixing bowl and serve immediately.

Pesto

INGREDIENTS

2 cups packed fresh basil leaves, packed

1 cup packed fresh baby spinach

2 cups freshly grated Parmesan cheese

¼ cup pine nuts

1 garlic clove

2 teaspoons fresh lemon juice

Salt and pepper, to taste

½ cup extra-virgin olive oil

DIRECTIONS

1. Place all of the ingredients, except for the olive oil, in a food processor and pulse until pureed.

2. Transfer the puree to a mixing bowl. While whisking, add the olive oil in a slow steam and work the mixture until emulsified.

Brunch Board

Skip the lines, bid the underwhelming Bloody Marys and overpriced eggs adieu, and take back Sunday with the help of this board.

A BREAKFAST SAUSAGE

If you have a local farm that sells meat, inquire about the availability of sausage, as their offering is guaranteed to be more flavorful than what's available at the store.

B JASPER HILL WEYBRIDGE

A soft cows' milk cheese that hails from Vermont, Weybridge's toasty flavor makes perfect sense on a morning-oriented board.

C BUTTERMILK WAFFLES

The slight tang of buttermilk helps this classic win over generation after generation.

D FRESH BERRIES

Go with a mix of whatever looks best at the market.

E COFFEE

Spiked, if you wish.

Buttermilk Waffles

YIELD: 4 Servings
ACTIVE TIME: 20 Minutes
TOTAL TIME: 30 Minutes

INGREDIENTS

2 cups all-purpose flour

2 tablespoons sugar

2 teaspoons baking powder

½ teaspoon kosher salt

2 cups buttermilk

8 tablespoons unsalted butter, melted

2 eggs

DIRECTIONS

1. Preheat a waffle iron. Place the flour, sugar, baking powder, and salt in a large bowl and whisk to combine.

2. Place the remaining ingredients in a separate mixing bowl, whisk to combine, and add the wet mixture to the dry mixture. Whisk until the mixture comes together as a smooth batter.

3. Working in batches, ladle the batter into the waffle iron and cook until browned and crispy.

Breakfast Sausage

YIELD: 4 Servings
ACTIVE TIME: 15 Minutes
TOTAL TIME: 15 Minutes

INGREDIENTS

2 tablespoons unsalted butter

8 oz. breakfast sausage links

DIRECTIONS

1. Place the butter in a large skillet and melt it over medium heat.

2. Add the sausage and cook, turning occasionally, until it is well browned all over and cooked through. Remove from the pan and serve immediately.

Buttermilk Waffles
see page 212

Dessert Board

Some elect to have charcuterie and cheese in place of dessert. I thought, "Why choose?" and combined the two.

A CANDIED BACON

You've had worse ideas than crumbling any leftovers of this over the frosting on a chocolate cake.

B CHOCOLATE-DIPPED STRAWBERRIES

As usual, chocolate manages to lift and be lifted by its partner.

C SKI QUEEN CARAMEL CHEESE

A Norwegian cheese with a truly incredible sweet, creamy flavor.

D BISCOTTI

Take the hint—brew some coffee to go along with this board.

E ALMONDS

Any will do, but the Marcona is always the best choice.

Chocolate–Dipped Strawberries

YIELD: 8 Servings
ACTIVE TIME: 10 Minutes
TOTAL TIME: 2 Hours and 10 Minutes

INGREDIENTS

2 pints of fresh strawberries

2 cups chocolate chips

DIRECTIONS

1. Rinse the strawberries well and pat them dry.

2. Fill a small saucepan halfway with water and bring it to a simmer. Place the chocolate chips in a heatproof bowl and place it over the simmering water. Stir occasionally until the chocolate is melted.

3. Dip each strawberry into the chocolate halfway, or completely, whichever you prefer. Line a baking sheet with parchment paper and place the strawberries on the sheet. Place in the refrigerator and chill for at least 2 hours before serving.

Candied Bacon

YIELD: 8 Servings
ACTIVE TIME: 10 Minutes
TOTAL TIME: 40 Minutes

INGREDIENTS

1 lb. thick-cut bacon

1 cup brown sugar

1 tablespoon black pepper

DIRECTIONS

1. Preheat the oven to 375°F. Place a wire rack in a rimmed baking sheet and place the bacon on the rack. Sprinkle the brown sugar over the bacon and gently pat it down with your fingers.

2. Sprinkle the pepper over the bacon and bake the bacon in the oven until the sugar has caramelized, about 25 minutes. Remove from the oven and serve warm or at room temperature.

Biscotti

INGREDIENTS

1 cup all-purpose flour

¾ teaspoon baking powder

Pinch of fine sea salt

¼ cup sugar

⅓ cup brown sugar

¼ cup extra-virgin olive oil

½ teaspoon cardamom

½ teaspoon cinnamon

¼ teaspoon ground ginger

⅛ teaspoon ground cloves

⅛ teaspoon freshly grated nutmeg

Zest of 1 orange

1 teaspoon pure vanilla extract

2 eggs

2 tablespoons Demerara sugar

DIRECTIONS

1. Preheat the oven to 350°F and line a baking sheet with parchment paper. Place all of the ingredients, except for the orange zest, vanilla, eggs, and Demerara sugar, in a mixing bowl and whisk to combine.

2. Add the orange zest, vanilla, and eggs and work the mixture by hand until it comes together as a dough.

3. Place the dough on the baking sheet and shape it into a rectangle that is about 5 inches wide. Sprinkle the Demerara sugar over the top and bake the biscotti until it is golden brown, about 20 minutes. Remove from the oven and let the biscotti cool. Leave the oven on.

4. Cut the biscotti as desired, lay them on the tray so that one of the cut sides is facing down, and bake for another 20 minutes, turning the biscotti over halfway through. Remove and let cool completely before serving.

From the Sea Board

Clean, simple, and fresh flavors are the focus of our final board, which is perfect for a small, intimate New Year's gathering beside a glass or two of bubbly.

A **OYSTERS**

These hail from the coast of Maine, but any of your favorites will work.

B **MIGNONETTE SAUCE**

This simple sauce is what fresh oysters cry out for.

C **SHRIMP COCKTAIL**

As with most things, homemade cocktail sauce is far better than store-bought.

D **SALMON ROE**

The oysters give you the sense of the sea. The roe gives you the suggestion of the delicate foam carried on its waves.

E **HORSERADISH HAVARTI CHEESE**

For those who shy away from spice, a dill Havarti will also work on this board.

F **CRÈME FRAÎCHE**

You can purchase at the store, or make by combining 1 cup of heavy cream and 1 tablespoon of buttermilk and let it rest at room temperature for 12 hours before storing in the refrigerator, where it will keep for up to 2 weeks.

G **NORI CRACKERS**

A dried, edible seaweed that crisps up beautifully.

H **KETTLE-COOKED POTATO CHIPS**

If you've never enjoyed caviar on a potato chip, you're welcome.

Shrimp Cocktail

YIELD: 4 Servings
ACTIVE TIME: 20 Minutes
TOTAL TIME: 1 Hour

INGREDIENTS

½ cup ketchup

2 tablespoons horseradish

2 tablespoons Worcestershire sauce

Juice of ½ lemon

1 teaspoon Old Bay seasoning

8 oz. large shrimp, shelled and deveined

DIRECTIONS

1. Place the ketchup, horseradish, Worcestershire sauce, and lemon juice in a bowl, stir to combine, and chill in the refrigerator for 1 hour before serving.

2. Prepare an ice water bath. Place water in a medium saucepan and bring it to a boil. Add the Old Bay and the shrimp and poach the shrimp until cooked through, about 5 minutes.

3. Shock the shrimp in the ice water and chill in the refrigerator until ready to serve.

Mignonette Sauce

YIELD: ½ Cup
ACTIVE TIME: 5 Minutes
TOTAL TIME: 5 Minutes

INGREDIENTS

½ cup red wine vinegar

1½ tablespoons minced shallot

½ teaspoon freshly cracked black pepper

DIRECTIONS

1. Place all of the ingredients in a bowl, stir to combine, and chill in the refrigerator for 1 hour before serving.

Nori Crackers

YIELD: 30 Crackers
ACTIVE TIME: 30 Minutes
TOTAL TIME: 45 Minutes

INGREDIENTS

1 egg

1 tablespoon water

3 spring roll wrappers

3 sheets of nori

6 tablespoons sesame seeds

4 cups canola oil

Salt, to taste

DIRECTIONS

1. Combine the egg and water and brush the spring roll wrappers with the egg wash. Place a sheet of nori on top of each wrapper and brush the nori with the egg wash. Sprinkle the sesame seeds on top and let rest for 10 minutes.

2. Place the oil in a Dutch oven and warm it to 300°F over medium heat. Cut each sheet into nine squares, place them in the oil, and fry until browned and crispy, about 5 minutes. Transfer to a paper towel–lined plate, season with salt, and serve.

Nori Crackers
see page 230

Metric Conversions

US MEASUREMENT	APPROXIMATE METRIC LIQUID MEASUREMENT	APPROXIMATE METRIC DRY MEASUREMENT
1 teaspoon	5 ml	5 g
1 tablespoon or ½ ounce	15 ml	14 g
1 ounce or ⅛ cup	30 ml	29 g
¼ cup or 2 ounces	60 ml	57 g
⅓ cup	80 ml	76 g
½ cup or 4 ounces	120 ml	113 g
⅔ cup	160 ml	151 g
¾ cup or 6 ounces	180 ml	170 g
1 cup or 8 ounces or ½ pint	240 ml	227 g
1½ cups or 12 ounces	350 ml	340 g
2 cups or 1 pint or 16 ounces	475 ml	454 g
3 cups or 1½ pints	700 ml	680 g
4 cups or 2 pints or 1 quart	950 ml	908 g

Index

About the Authors

When Derek Bissonnette was 16 he landed his first kitchen gig, at a bakery in Searsport, Maine. He went on to study baking and pastry at the Culinary Institute of America, graduating in 2000. He was hired as the pastry chef at the estimable White Barn Inn in Kennebunk, Maine, jumped to the renowned Inn at Little Washington in rural Virginia, and then joined the kitchen at the elegant English countryside hotel, The Summer Lodge Country House Hotel and Spa. In 2009, he returned to Maine and the White Barn, where he was promoted to executive chef in 2015. After Bissonnette took over the White Barn kitchen, he started toting a camera to work to create a visual record of dishes he and his staff came up with. Photography clicked with him, and in 2017, he gave up his apron to pursue photography full time. He is also the author of *Soup: The Ultimate Cookbook* and *Dumplings*. Find out more at dbfoodphoto.com.

Gabrielle Cote attended the prestigious Culinary Institute of America (CIA), where she earned a degree in Bakery and Pastry Arts. Two days after graduating, she landed a pastry internship at the legendary White Barn Inn in Kennebunkport, Maine, and quickly made her way up to pastry chef, overseeing the entire pastry and bakery program at that landmark establishment. Currently, she is sous chef and pastry program manager at Earth at Hidden Pond in Kennebunkport.

About Cider Mill Press Book Publishers

Good ideas ripen with time. From seed to harvest, Cider Mill Press brings fine reading, information, and entertainment together between the covers of its creatively crafted books. Our Cider Mill bears fruit twice a year, publishing a new crop of titles each spring and fall.

"Where Good Books Are Ready for Press"

Visit us online at
cidermillpress.com
or write to us at
PO Box 454
12 Spring St.
Kennebunkport, Maine 04046